SAINT MARTIN DE PORRES

By REV.
LAWRENCE G. LOVASIK, S.V.D.
Divine Word Missionary

CPSIA   February 2016   10 9 8 7 6 5 4 3 2 1   L/P

St. Joseph Kids' Books

CATHOLIC BOOK PUBLISHING CORP.
New York

NIHIL OBSTAT: Daniel V. Flynn, J.C.D., *Censor Librorum*
IMPRIMATUR: ✠ James P. Mahoney, D.D., *Vicar General, Archdiocese of New York*

Peru, in South America, was discovered in 1527.

Printed in China

Martin's Place of Birth—Lima

THE country of Peru in South America was discovered in 1529 by Francisco Pizarro, a Spaniard. On January 6, 1529, the Feast of the Epiphany or the Three Kings, he founded the capital city of Peru and called it "City of the Kings."

Later, the city took the name of the valley where it was located—Lima. Since that time it has been known as the city of Lima. It was the capital of the first vice-royalty begun in America.

After the discovery of Peru, many Spanish people came to bring Spanish culture to America. One of them was John de Porres, a nobleman from Alcantara. He had been born in Burgos but his ancestors were from Cordoba, Spain.

John came to the New World as the Governor of Panama. On the way, he stopped at Lima.

Martin's Father and Mother

MARTIN'S mother was a beautiful black woman, born in Panama, who traveled about to earn her living as an entertainer. This lovely free-woman, Anna Velazques, attracted the notice of young John de Porres.

Because of the racism that was part of that age, marriage was out of the question. From this union came first a son, born December 9, 1579, and named Martin. He was baptized in the church of St. Sebastian where St. Rose of Lima was baptized six years earlier.

Martin was black like his mother. John's love for Anna remained and she bore him a daughter they named Joan, born two years after Martin.

Anna Velazques fell in love with John de Porres.

Martin's Childhood

FOR a while things went fairly well, but then John was sent to Guayaquil, the seaport of Equador. He forgot about Anna and their two children.

We are told that during this time Anna was rather poor: she would send Martin to the store and he would end up giving the money to the poor. Though punished, he felt that it was his duty to give to the poor. Of his early childhood we know little except that he liked to visit churches.

John returned to Lima for a visit when Martin was eight. He took his son and daughter back to Guayaquil with him and hired a tutor to teach them. But this lasted only two years and the children were sent back to Lima, Martin to his mother and Joan to an uncle, James de Miranda.

Money was given to Anna for Martin's education. John wanted him to learn a trade.

Joan was born two years after Martin.

Martin Learns a Profession as a Teenager

SO the young teenager came to work for Manuel de Rivero, a barber-surgeon, and this seemed to be Martin's choice. In those days, bloodletting was a popular medical treatment and this was done by barber-surgeons. They cut hair and trimmed beards; they set and amputated bones. As doctors, they gave herbs to the sick for fever.

Martin was a bright boy. He quickly learned all that Manuel could teach him.

Martin served Mass first and then went to work. At home in the evening he went to his room and prayed. One time the landlady peeked in the keyhole and there was Martin on his knees, his arms outstretched and his eyes on the Crucifix.

Whatever money Martin made was divided: some to his mother, the rest to the poor.

When Martin was fifteen, his father came from Panama for a visit to Lima. He made sure that Anna was cared for.

Vocation to the Religious Life

THIS left Martin free to follow a life of his own. He wanted to enter a monastery. Anna and John were pleased.

His father was disappointed to hear that his son wanted to be a brother and not a priest. But Martin was firm and would not change his mind.

Martin served Mass first and then went to work.

Martin Enters a Monastery

MARTIN entered the Dominican monastery of the Holy Rosary in Lima as a servant. He felt that he was unworthy of being a brother.

One day the superior of the monastery took some precious objects from the monastery to sell, since money was needed badly.

When Martin heard, he fell on his knees and begged him not to sell the valuable objects but to sell him. He said he deserved to be treated as a slave and pledged to serve a new master also. The superior told him: "Go back to the monastery. You are not for sale."

During this time there were four Saints in Lima. St. John Massias, a Dominican brother and Martin's good friend, worked in the monastery of St. Mary Magdalene. St. Turibius, the second Archbishop of Lima, died when Martin was thirty years old. St. Rose of Lima was six years older than Martin. Martin was present when St. Francis Solano, a Franciscan, died.

Martin Becomes a Brother

ONE day slipped into the next with Martin growing in holiness and working hard to serve others. After Martin had spent about nine years in the monastery as a "donado," a servant, the superiors urged him to a closer union with the Dominican Order.

In 1603 Martin made his vows as a full-fledged Dominican, a brother with the vocation of prayer and work.

Martin made his vows as a Dominican brother.

Martin — a Good Religious

MARTIN'S life was simple and he followed the life in the monastery like a Saint. There was hardly any furniture in his room. His bed was a few planks with a bundle of straw and a piece of wood for a pillow.

He did have the pictures of the Blessed Virgin Mary, St. Dominic, and St. Vincent Ferrer. But he rarely used the bed. At night he could be found in prayer in the chapel, or elsewhere performing acts of penance.

He wore a hairshirt and a chain around his waist, fasted often, and during Lent took only bread and water. On the three last days of Holy Week, he ate nothing. He never ate meat.

Martin's clothing was always what was patched or thrown away. Only once did he get a new habit, and when someone noticed it, he said: "This is the habit I am to be buried in."

Under obedience he was commanded to reveal some details of his life. He fulfilled the vow of obedience with a prompt, joyful, and strong will.

At night Martin could be found in prayer in the chapel.

Martin's Battle with the Devil

MARTIN had to fight with the devil who not only tempted him but even laughed at him and punished him as he did St. John Vianney.

Francis de la Torre, an officer of the guard, tells us that during the night he heard Martin cry out: "What have you come here for, you troublemaker? What are you looking for? This is not your room. Get out!"

There was much noise. Martin was treated harshly. He was rolled back and forth on the floor and hurled against the wall. He was hurt and moaned under the blows. Then a flame burst out in the cell and Francis helped Martin put it out. In the morning there was no sign of fire or damage in the cell but Martin was bruised.

The Novice Master, Father Andrew, told the novices: "This mulatto is a Saint, and should be venerated as a Saint. Last night he had a dreadful battle with the devil and conquered him. "

Martin, the Friend of the Sick

IN the monastery Martin had several tasks. He was assistant infirmarian and cared for the sick. He had charge of the monastery wardrobe and worked in the field.

An epidemic broke out in Lima. There were 60 sick people in the monastery because the two hospitals in the city were filled. He took two sick people to his own cell.

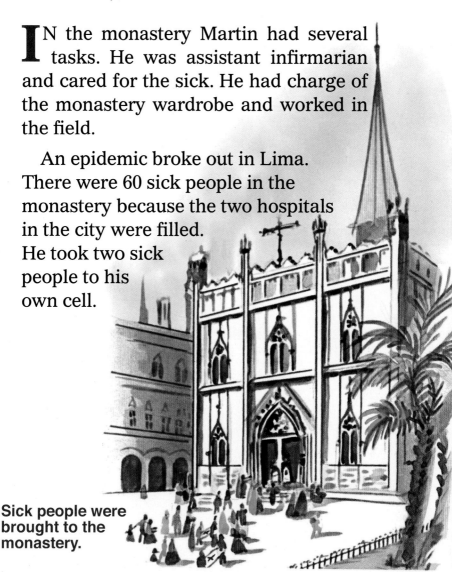

Sick people were brought to the monastery.

Martin carried the sick to his sister's home.

16

Joan Helps Martin with the Sick

WHEN the monks asked how he could bring the sick to the cloister, which was off limits to the people, Brother Martin replied: "There are no cloisters for the sick."

Martin was full of love for God and kindness toward the sick. He was very zealous in his work. If some of the sick showed no patience with him, he served them kneeling.

Brother Martin carried sick people in his arms to the house of his sister, Joan, who was his generous helper. Long hours in the day and night were spent at the side of the suffering sick people.

Miracles Worked by Martin

MARTIN'S work with the sick gave rise to many stories of his closeness to God and what we would call miracles. There is the story of Louis Gutierrez, a seventeen-year-old novice who received a gash on his hand. He came to Martin in pain from an infection and fever. Martin put some herbs on the wound, bandaged it, and made the Sign of the Cross over it. The next morning all signs of infection were gone.

Father Peter's leg was gravely infected and the plan was to cut it off the next day. Martin removed the bandages and put his hand on the diseased leg. It was healed!

Father Thomas, an old man who had been sick, was anointed and then died. He was cold when Martin came to his room and people were preparing the body for burial. Martin prayed, put his mouth to Father Thomas's ear, and called him by name. Color came to his face and he came back to life.

One day Brother Martin found a man a few steps from the monastery door, cut and bleeding to death. At once he took him to the monastery and cared for him.

The Church honors Martin as a saint, not because of wondrous works people say he had, but because of his love which made him a friend to every person he met.

Martin prayed for cures and his prayers were answered.

Martin's Love for the Poor and Helpless

On the road Martin planted trees for the poor.

MARTIN had a great love for the poor. He tilled a plot of land and sowed a garden for the poor. The garden yielded crops to feed the poor. On a road in the country Martin planted fruit trees so the poor would have something to eat.

"Father of All"

EVEN those who were once rich and were too proud to beg were helped by Martin in such a way that they were not ashamed. Prisoners were helped; he brought them food and clothing. He was called "Father of the Poor," "Father of Charity," and "Father of All."

There was a problem about abandoned children and orphans who had no home. So Martin begged and planned. Soon there was a home and school for orphans dedicated to the Holy Cross. Not only did he start it but he made sure they had the best teachers.

He would spend much of his time with the children and helped them when they were ill. They all loved him because he was so friendly and kind. His own soul was like that of a child in its simplicity and innocence.

Martin's Love for Animals

BROTHER Martin was very cheerful and very simple. He loved God with a great love. He loved all human beings and all creatures very much, because God had made all.

All kinds of stories grew up about Martin and his dealings with animals.

Martin loved animals because God made them.

One day he found some mice among the clothes. The story is that he took one of them in his hands and said: "My little brother mouse, I don't know whether you are the guilty one for all the damage done in the sacristy and in the wardrobe. Today you and your friends will have to leave the monastery."

Later all the mice gathered around Brother Martin, and he placed them in a basket. He brought them to an open field and let them loose. He brought them food.

For eighteen years the monastery dog had been serving the monks. One day Brother Martin found it bleeding from a neck wound. He took care of the dog for a week, and it was cured.

One day Martin was passing by a stable and saw a mule lying down on the ground. The poor animal had a broken leg and was dying. Full of pity, Martin said to it: "Creature of God, get up and be cured!" The mule got up—completely cured. He started to run around.

Martin's Love for Jesus

MARTIN came to the monastery to be a servant of all to imitate the example of Jesus, Who said He came into this world to serve and not to be served. For the love of Jesus he did all his works of love for others. He loved all, especially those who were in need, the poor, the sick, the suffering, slaves and helpless children.

Most of all, he loved Jesus in the Blessed Sacrament. Holy Mass was the center of his daily life. Holy Communion was his way of loving Jesus most and of making his soul holy. Free hours would be spent before the tabernacle.

God granted to Martin the gift of prayer. His prayers were full of love, faith, humility, and perseverance. He was sometimes so close to God in prayer that his body was lifted in midair, while his face touched the Crucifix. He lived more in heaven than on earth, because his entire life was dedicated to God through prayer and acts of charity.

Martin prayed before the tabernacle and the cross.

25

Martin loved the
Blessed Virgin
Mary.

26

Martin's Love for Mary

MARTIN had a very great devotion to the Blessed Virgin Mary. He prayed fervently to her, carrying one Rosary around his neck and another at his side so in free moments he would finger the beads.

His devotion to Mary was rewarded with visions of her and she taught him to love God more. He loved Mary as his dearest Mother, for he knew that in this way he could be more like Jesus.

When the Spaniards celebrated the national holiday, Martin covered Mary's altar with flowers, which he often had in the monastery chapel. He often prayed before her picture in his monastery cell.

The Blessed Virgin appeared to him and talked with him.

Martin felt a son's love for the Mother of God. She was close to him during his life and especially at his death.

Martin Goes to God

E VERY autumn Martin suffered an attack of quartan fever, a type of malaria, and so no one was surprised in the Fall of 1639 when Martin became ill. But fears arose when he told certain ones that he would die.

He told Brother Anthony: "Don't weep, brother, because perhaps I will be more useful there in heaven than here."

Filled with love for God, he asked for the Sacraments and said: "This is the end of my pilgrimage on earth. The Blessed Virgin, St. Joseph, St. Dominic, St. Catherine, and St. Vincent Ferrer are here with me."

He looked up and asked pardon of all.

As was the custom in the monastery, the priests and brothers sang the "Hail, Holy Queen" and then one intoned the Creed. At the words, "and He became man" Martin gave his pure soul to God. It was 9:00 A.M. on the 3rd of November, 1639. He was a few days short of fifty years of age.

Word of Martin's death spread through Lima and very soon crowds of people came to see him for the last time. Miracles worked on the spot brought even more people. To avoid a riot, Martin was buried the next night.

Martin gave his pure soul to God.

Martin Is Declared a Saint

ANGELS rejoiced when Martin reached his heavenly home. But on earth the rich and the poor, the sick and the prisoners, the widows and the orphans—the whole city of Lima cried for its benefactor and friend.

The highest dignitaries, both civil and religious, were his pallbearers. Everyone wanted to honor this holy man.

God's greatest gift to Martin was the grace to love God with all his heart and soul and strength, and to love his neighbor for the love of God. He showed this charity all through his lifetime.

Martin's closeness to Christ and the miracles he worked prompted the bishops to start an investigation into his life and holiness.

Finally, the humble brother who looked for so little in life was beatified in 1837. Many miracles followed as he became more popular.

Pope John XXIII declared him a Saint of the Catholic Church on May 6, 1962.

Angels rejoiced when Martin reached his heavenly home.

A visitor to Lima can visit the shrine of St. Martin de Porres in the Dominican church there. Above the altar is his skull in crystal and close by is that of St. Rose of Lima.

Holy Mother Church celebrates the feast of St. Martin de Porres on November 3.

People turn to him for help. In heaven angels are filled with joy. From heaven Martin still continues to be kind to people on earth.

The Prayer of the Church in Honor of Saint Martin

LORD,
   You led Martin de Porres
by a life of humility
to eternal glory.

May we follow his example
and be exalted with him
in the kingdom of heaven.

Grant this through our Lord
Jesus Christ, Your Son,
Who lives and reigns with You
and the Holy Spirit,
one God, for ever and ever.
Amen.